A Baby's Coming to Your House!

WRITTEN BY

Shelley Moore Thomas

PHOTOGRAPHED BY

Eric Futran

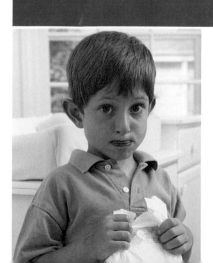

Also by Shelley Moore Thomas and Eric Futran:
Somewhere Today: A Book of Peace

For Caledonia, the baby who came to our house.
— S. M. T.

To Rachael and Jake, my babies, who are growing
up much too fast. — E. F.

Thanks to Shanita, Jimmy, and Jimi Daniel Akintonde; Greg, Jessica,
and Ryan Poulet; Anita Blanchard-Nesbitt and Maxine Nesbitt; Rob and
Liz Caya; Lynn and Carolyn Brezina; Ruth and Jack Curran; John and
Abby Leonard; Shelly, Joshua, Julia, Jacob, and Noah Masur; Patti,
Michael, Lucas, and Matthew Quilling; Alan, C. J., Michael, and Dana
Hatter; Theri Raby, Jack Newsom, Emilio Raby-Newsom, and Raquel
Raby-Newsom; Becky and Andy Galler; Margaret and Patricia Duffy;
Young and Emily Varua; Yvonne, Stephanie, and Katherine Tinsley;
Christy, Stephen, John, and Colleen King; Ava, Ella, and Lana Berry;
Suzanne Chevrier, Jim Dore, Connor Chevrier Dore, and Abigail Chevrier
Dore; and Yvonne, Isa, and Jakob Kaminsky for giving their time to take
part in this book.

Thanks also to Joshua M. Masur for his photographs of his daughter
and twin sons and to Lazar's Juvenile Furniture, Chicago, Illinois.

Library of Congress Cataloging-in-Publication Data

Thomas, Shelley Moore.
A baby's coming to your house! / by Shelley Moore Thomas;
photographs by Eric Futran.
p. cm.
ISBN 0-8075-0502-1
1. Infants — Juvenile literature. [1. Babies.] I. Futran, Eric, ill.   II. Title.
HQ774 .T48 2001   305.232 — dc21   00-010205

When a baby comes to your house,
there are many changes.

The first thing you notice
is your mommy's tummy.
It gets bigger,
and her lap gets smaller.
Sometimes her tummy moves
in funny ways.
Sometimes it even kicks you!
Don't worry.
It is only the baby dancing.

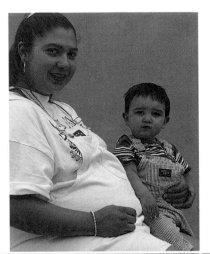

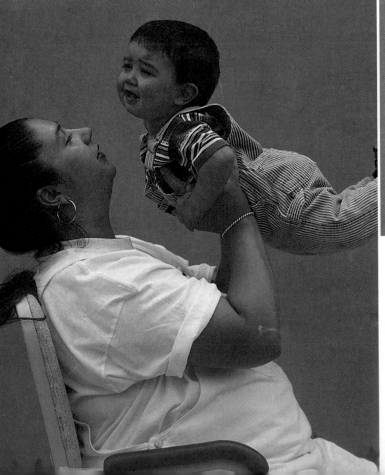

When a baby comes to your house,
it comes with lots of furniture and things.
There are cribs and swings and strollers.
There are highchairs and playpens and car seats.
There are toys and teddies and baby-sized blankets.
Who would think that a person so small
would need so much stuff?

Babies also have lots and lots
of teeny little clothes.
The clothes look like
they would fit
a doll
or a kitten
or a puppy.
But don't dress your pet
in the baby's pajamas.
It will make your mommy mad.
The pet won't like it much, either!

Then, one day, after things
are ready for the baby,
the baby will be ready, too!
Most of the time,
mommies go to the hospital
to have their babies.
(But sometimes a mommy
will have her baby
right there in her very own home.)

Sometimes parents adopt babies.
They may go far away to get a child.
Maybe even to China.

When a baby comes to your house,
it might be a sister
or it might be a brother.

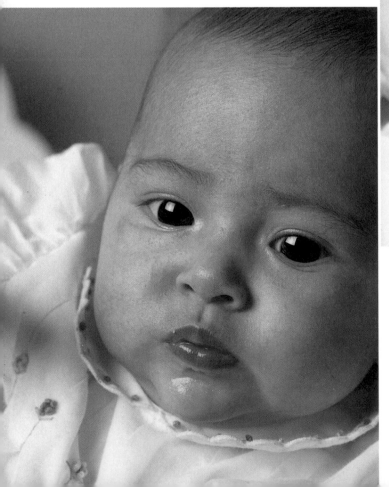

Sometimes you get twins!
Then you can have two sisters
or two brothers
or one sister and one brother.
Sometimes mommies and daddies
bring home several babies.
But usually there is just one.
A boy or a girl.

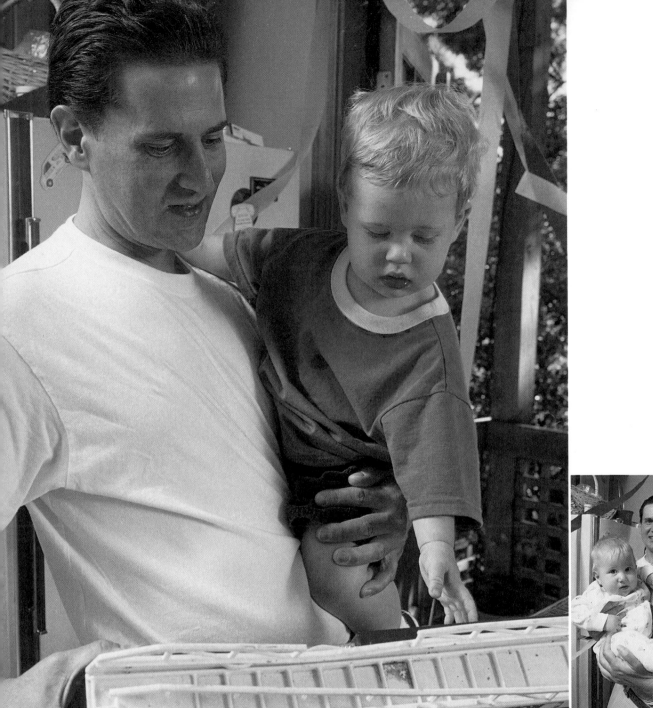

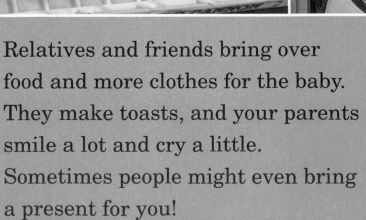

Relatives and friends bring over
food and more clothes for the baby.
They make toasts, and your parents
smile a lot and cry a little.
Sometimes people might even bring
a present for you!

People will be passing that baby around
and saying silly things like
"Aren't you a cutie wootie?"
or
"You're just an itty, bitty, wittle thing."
Grownups talk funny around babies.
So get used to it.

There will be lots of cameras flashing,
so smile!

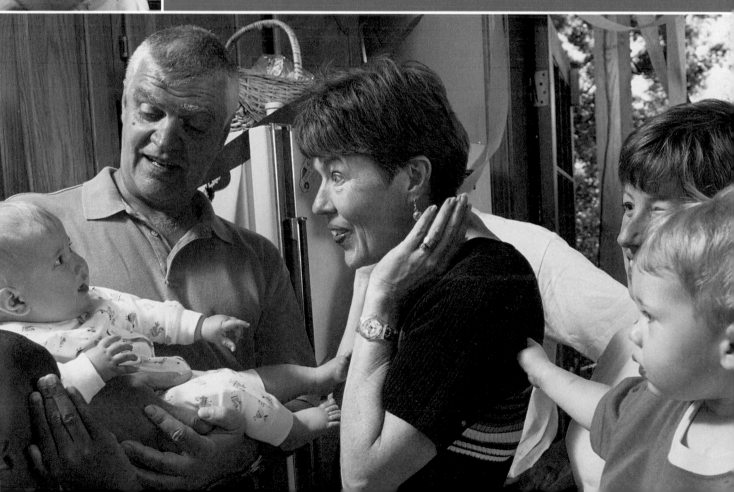

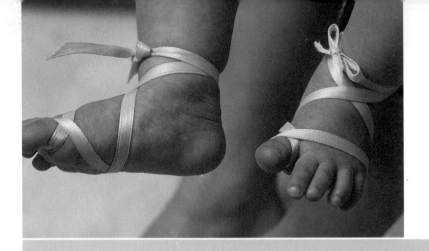

When your house is calm and quiet,
your parents will
let you hold the baby.
Don't bounce it or pinch it,
or you won't get
to hold it very much.

If you sit very still,
you can feel when the baby
breathes.
In and out, in and out.
Sometimes the baby will make
small, quiet noises.
This is sweet.

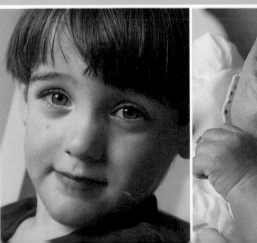

Sometimes the baby will make
loud, crying noises
that are not so sweet.
Get used to the crying.
Crying is baby language for
"Feed me!" or "Hold me!"
or "Change my diaper!"

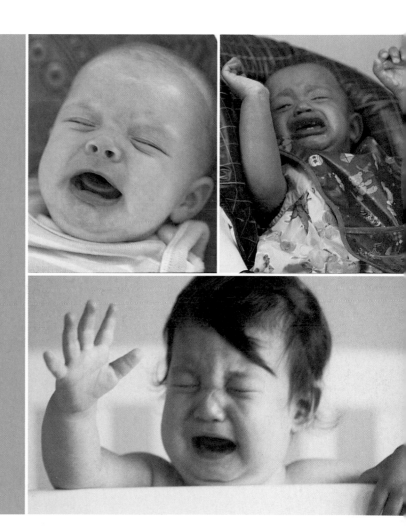

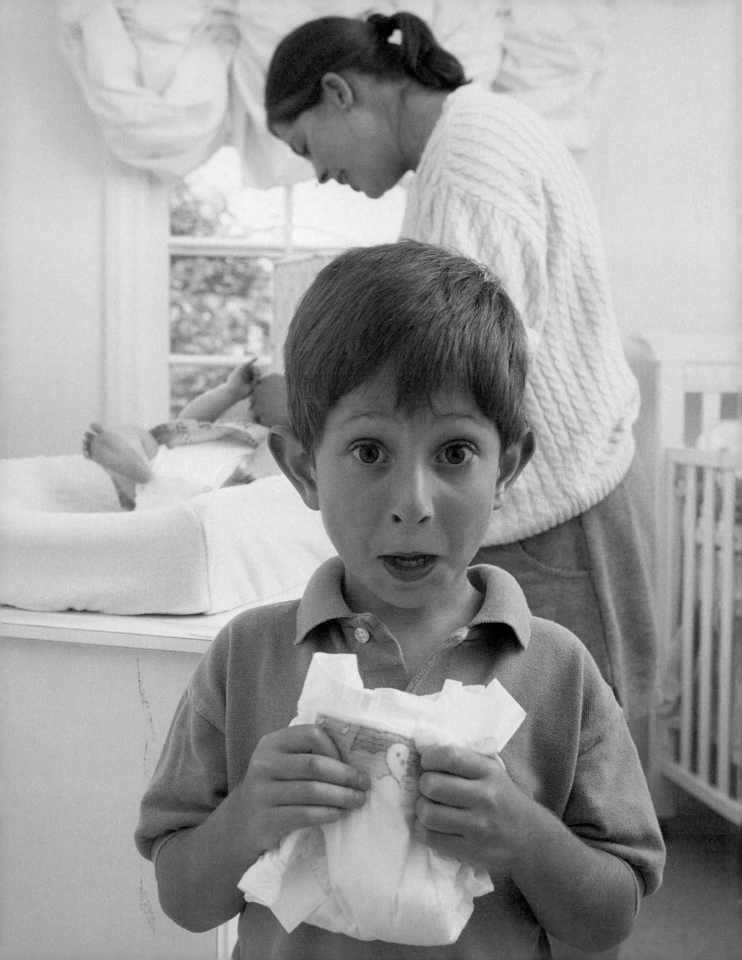

Speaking of changing diapers,
when a baby comes to your house,
you will have to learn about diapers.
Get ready.
Your parents are going to ask YOU
to take the dirty one away.
Be careful!
If you go too fast,
you may drop it.
Yuck.
If you go too slow,
you have to smell it.
Yuck.
You have to walk
just the right speed
with a messy diaper.

Sometimes it is a good idea
to go outside
when the baby starts to smell,
just to be safe.

Houses with babies
sometimes must be very quiet.
Grownups say, "Shhh!" a lot
when a baby comes
because babies need their sleep.
So don't yell around a baby.
If you wake it,
it will be fussy and cranky.
So will your mommy.

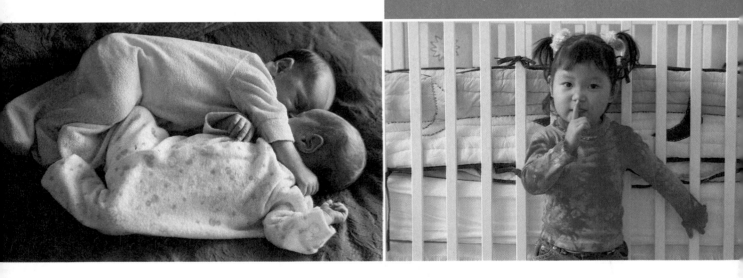

Babies don't eat the same food
as the rest of the family.
No cheesy pizza.
No chocolate-covered ice cream bars.
No crisp red apples.
Just smashed-up, mushed-up food.
And, of course, milk.

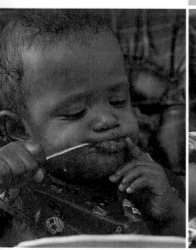
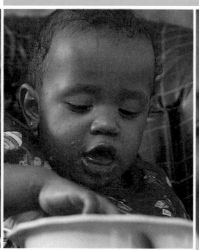

When a baby comes to your house,
your parents will be holding it a lot.
They will be looking at that baby
and checking on that baby.
They will be snuggling it
and caring for it.

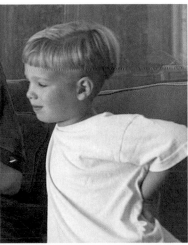

But don't worry.
Even though you are bigger,
your mommy and daddy
will always have time
to look at you and check on you,
to snuggle you and care for you.

When a baby comes to your house, you will have to teach it many things.

It will not know about the blue sky
or birthday candles
or how to blow bubbles.

It will not know about finding
smooth, perfect shells on a sandy beach
or sharing a special toy on a rainy day.
It will not know how to spin like a ballerina
or swing like a monkey in a tree.

It will only know about milk.

You and your family
will have to teach the baby
everything it will nccd to get along.
So make sure you teach it
all about love
and hugs
and laughter
and silly baby kisses.

Then you will be very happy
when a baby comes to your house.